Alois Irlmaier g

WAR

in

2021...?

Alois Irlmaier gave signs of this
as far back as 1959...

Note:

This book is printed in a larger font for greater readability.

Bibliographical information of the German National Library: The German National Library lists this publication in the German National Bibliography; detailed bibliographical information can be found on the internet at www.dnb.de.

Production and publication:
BoD – Books on Demand, Norderstedt

ISBN 978-3-7504-9958-4

Table of Contents

Preface

I'm Tayala Léha, a healer and author with
the gift of medium since birth. How did
this small book come about?

On 30 April 2020, I just fell over in front of
the garden gate at home. I couldn't move
or talk. I couldn't even open my eyes... In
my mind's eye, I saw a white light coming
towards me and a male voice asked me
lovingly THE QUESTION: "Do you want to
come with me?". My longing was SO
strong in this moment, that I simply said
"yes". But the soft voice whispered to me:
"I still need you on Earth...".

Then why did you ask me if I wanted to go? Immediately, images flashed before me. I had visions that showed me WHY I was genuinely still needed with my "slightly different skills"... As the white light faded, my physical weakness miraculously disappeared within a few minutes.

At the kitchen table the same evening, I was prompted to pick up my mobile and google a specific "key word". I actually felt too exhausted to do it but the voice in my head was so unrelenting that I did what it asked me...

I was led to the predictions of ALOIS IRLMAIER...

I had never heard of this man until that day.

Who was Alois Irlmaier?

Alois Irlmaier was a well builder and clairvoyant and lived from 1894 to 1959.
Even during his lifetime, his psychic abilities were very sought after. Konrad Adenauer himself is said to have paid Alois Irlmaier a visit.

Back in his home town, everybody WAS AWARE of Alois Irlmaier's CAPABILITIES. They took his predictions seriously and this saved many people's lives because he was able to accurately predict bomb attacks.

Even in front of the District Court in Laufen, he freed himself from the accusation of "trickery" by PROVING what he could do. In the court judgment of 4 September 1950, you can still to this day read about the gifts he demonstrated. (1*)

Over the ten years up to his death in 1959, he warned of a third world war, which would befall German completely unexpectedly... But: there were signs!

The SIGNS of the Third World War

According to Alois Irlmaier there will be the following signs IN GERMANY:

- *First comes prosperity like never before!*
- *Then there is a decline in faith like never before.*
- *Then moral corruption like never before.*
- *Then a large amount of colourful strangers arrive in the country.*
- *Money loses more and more of its value.*
- *Soon after, a revolution ensues.*
- *Then overnight, the Russians invade the West.*

...We can buy everything our hearts desire.

...Who still really believes in God these days?

...Pornos, one night stands and swinger clubs - pure "moral corruption"?

...2015 – the refugee crisis.

...Is our money LOSING value due to the coronavirus crisis?

..."Revolution" - in Spring 2020, the people took to the streets, not only in Germany...

...One year, in the midsummer period, the Russians will attack the West completely unexpectedly.

He didn't give exact dates but some cornerstones that people should watch out for:

***

"The war will break out at a time when people are paying with small cardboard lids and talking with small, black boxes that also give them answers."

I doubt that people knew about credit cards and smartphones in 1959...

***

He is reported to have told a young nurse at the Caritas hospital (she must have been about 18 years old at the time): "Miss, you will survive the greatest revolution.".

This lady must now be around 88 years old. How long does she have left to live???

***

The war will break out in the midsummer of a year with a very warm winter...

Last winter (2019/2020) was actually very warm for a "really wintry" Germany. What will the next winter be like?

***

Irlmaier said: "The trouble will travel the world!". Other clairvoyants call this sign the *"global crisis"*, that should immediately precede the war...

What does "TROUBLE" mean?

I looked it up...

Difficulty, problems, public unrest, distress, anxiety, grief, pain, suffering, turbulence.

The CORONAVIRUS CRISIS is a global crisis, that has caused "trouble" in every sense of the word in many countries across our world - or, at least, that's my interpretation...

Course of the War

In the midsummer of one year (presumably the end of July/beginning of August), the war is meant to come as a complete shock for everyone: *"After the third murder of a high-ranking person, the war will start overnight."*. Then *"OVERNIGHT, the Russians will invade the West", completely shocking everyone.* In Speyer, for example, the war will allegedly start one night between Friday and Saturday between midnight and 2 am...

Alois Irlmaier sees a THREE. *"Is it three days, three weeks or three months?"*. Since the "three days of darkness" will supposedly end this war in late autumn, the war will presumably last three months...

"From the Donau to the Rhine, everything will be covered in smoke." Retreat south of the Donau and west of the Rhine! That's where it will be safer tha in the rest of Germany, foresees Irlmaier.

For over a year, anyone who enters a wide stretch from the *Golden City* (Prague?) to the bay by the sea is said to die. **"Everything and everyone dies, even the worm 30 feet under the ground."**.

Poison? To be assumed. Thousands of combat drones can easily get the deadly matter *"out of the African sand"* on the *"planes without people"*.

"A single plane coming from the east, throws an object into the great water. It rises out of the water like a single object towering over everything before falling down again. Everything will be immersed." A hydrogen bomb can do exactly that! According to the prediction, this flood should immerse large parts of Belgium, Holland, Denmark, German and possibly northern France. It will be a flood that nobody in an area that is, according to the prophecy, high risk can escape. The southern part of the England will slide into the water…

Frankfurt, Landau an der Isar, Hamburg, Berlin, Karlsruhe, Cologne, Koblenz, Landshut, Nuremberg, Passau, Regensburg and Stuttgart are predicted to be at great danger during the war! He predicts that Munich, Lindau am Bodensee, the "Saurüssel", the east of the Bavarian Alps, the Allgäu and "Watzmann to Wendelstein" (mountains) will be **"relatively safe"** (apart from civil war-like riots and huge flows of refugees).

The Three Days of Darkness

Irlmaier claims that the war will end with "three days of darkness". More people in Germany will die in these 72 hours than the total of the first and second world war together. Lots of renowned prophets from various corners of the world and centuries have predicted this "three days of darkness" - mostly in connection with a war that will "be led from East to West".

Is the "three days of darkness" a natural catastrophe? It sounds like it because it is predicted for the entire northern hemisphere. Can people protect themselves and, if so, how?

Alois Irlmaier gives concrete tips:
- It is expected to start on a very cold night in late Autumn. People will hear thunder and should then TIGHTLY close all doors and windows.
- Tape the windows with black paper and don't look out. *"People who look out will die!"*.
- Don't let anybody in, no matter how much they beg.

- "Deadly dust" will circulate outside. People who breathe in the dust will get a cramp and die.
- People should light a sacred candle and pray. There will be a power cut.
- People should stockpile canned and dry food, such as honey and rice.

"First the war and then another extensive natural catastrophe will hit the whole northern hemisphere?" What nonsense!" - you might be tempted to say... But if you take a closer look at the available literature and read extensively in all directions, you will quickly find out: all roads lead to Rome... In short, the prophecies are genuinely possible! Obviously, that doesn't make the prophecy a certainty... What should we do now? Believe? Or are we best not believing? That seems to be a key question that could determine the fate of each and every one of us...

Cassandra Syndrome

That all seems UNBELIEVABLE? You're not alone in thinking that! Even I can NOT IMAGINE such a course of events. But, even if you cannot imagine that something like this would happen, sometimes such things happen ANYWAY!

Cassandra, the daughter of the Trojan King Priam, was a respected priestess and seeress. Everybody ignored her warning not to bring the "Trojan horse" (which the Greeks had left on the beach) into the interior of the city walls as a victory trophy. Even Cassandra's father didn't believe her warning and so the Troja was doomed... Even to this day, we still call it "Cassandra Syndrome" when people don't give any credit to a prophecy simply because they CANNOT IMAGINE it happening.

Alois Irlmaier emphatically warned of a third world war up until his death. On his deathbed, he said that he was actually happy because he wouldn't have to live through it. HE BELIEVED WHAT HE SAW... What do you do?

Sometimes it's hard to recognise
what's "real"...

Further Literature

If you have digested this first horror so far, I would now like to recommend books to you, so that you can INFORM yourself! You can find some information online. You can find detailed information on the various topics in the following books (in German):

- "Alois Irlmaier - Der Brunnenbauer von Freilassing. Sein Leben und seine Voraussagen." (Wolfgang Johannes Bekh)

- "Alois Irlmaier - Ein Mann sagt, was er sieht" (Stephan Berndt)

- "Zukunft des Abendlandes? Eine Untersuchung von Prophezeiungen." (Alexander Gann)

- "Countdown Weltkrieg 3.0 - Das Erscheinen der letzten Vorzeichen" (Stephan Berndt)

- "Prophezeiungen zum Dritten Weltkrieg" (Manfred Böckl)

- "Prophezeiungen zur Zukunft Europas und reale Ereignisse" (Stephan Berndt)

- "3 Tage im Spätherbst" (Stephan Berndt)

- "Refugium. Sichere Gebiete nach Alois Irlmaier und anderen Sehern." (Stephan Berndt)

- "Neustart: Visionen und Prophezeiungen über Europa und Deutschland nach Crash, Krieg und Finsternis" (Stephan Berndt)

Also, a good read in relation to this:

"Das Lied der Linde"
Prophecies for Germany.

Which Countries Will Be Affected?

According to Irlmaier and other European prophets, the following countries will be involved in the war (among others) (2*):

- **Germany** will be the "main battleground": especially between the Danube and the Rhine and after the bombing, the whole of Northern Germany to Hanover and up to and including Greater Berlin will be flooded - including Aachen, Cologne and the entire Rhine-Main area.

- **The Czech Republic** (particularly at risk): Bohemia and the city of Prague, which is said to be completely destroyed). Irlmaier said: *"Poor Bohemia, poor Prague!"*.

- **Austria** (Vienna, Linz and other towns and regions)

- **Belgium** (the flood caused by the bomb is expected to immerse a vast area! Bruges should be relatively safe in the war.)

- **Holland** (a large part of the country is

expected to be immersed by the flood caused by the bombs)

- Denmark (the flood caused by the bomb is expected to immerse a vast area here too!)

- **Finland** (Russia retreats via Finland *Sweden* and *Norway.*)

- Sweden (Umeå, Östersund, Härnösand, Göteborg, Malmö, Falsterbo, Hässleholm, Stockholm, Västervik, Söderköping, Norrköping, Nyköping, Örebro, Hallsberg, Gävle, Borlänge are expected to be severely damaged.)

-   **Italy** (unfortunately, too little information, but the coastal regions are at a great threat.)

- **France** (Marseille should sink into the see, lots of battles in Lyon, Strasbourg and Paris, the coastal regions in the Mediterranean areas are to be avoided.)

- **England** (due to the flood caused by the bombs between the mainland and the island, southern England is said to "slide down into the sea...".)

...via Alaska "*yellow people*" are said to invade **Canada** and the **US**. *"But the masses will retaliate."* claims Irlmaier.

So which countries won't be involved in the war...? And how? We won't find an answer to that today or here. I personally wonder what will annoy those in power in Russia so much to the point that they start a war. Irlmaier sees an attack on a high-ranking politician that triggers the war.
People react with emotions and politicians aren't immune to this. I think that nobody starts a war lightly. There is always something behind it...

In a nutshell: the prophecies "stand". You don't need to tell me that this all sound UNBELIEVABLE. But the predictions of Alois Irlmaier (Germany), Anton Johansson (Norway), Birger Claesson (Sweden) and many other prophets are a warning to us!

Practical Tips

How do you approach an event that you can`t evaluate? Difficult...

But what we can guess for sure: Supermarkets, pharmacies, petrol stations, power grids, water supply – all of this would be paralysed in times of war. What then? Are you prepared for such an event? In my opinion, the clear answer for most people is: NO. How then...?

So, what can you do so that you don't go into such a crisis situation completely unprepared? Being informed is important! Only people who are informed can prepare themselves...

However, if you read how this war is supposed to go, you may be wondering whether it is even possible to protect yourself.

So, ultimately the point for me is when our time is up, our time is up. Even if you're not convinced, it's always a possibility!

Burying your head in the stand – that is, at least in my opinion, not an option...

So, I recommend PREVENTION, which you can do PRACTICALLY, but which of course only makes sense if you are not in a particularly vulnerable area.

1. Secure information reception with WORLD RECEIVER (be independent of the power grid!)
2. Place a bag with all important documents and some money near the apartment door
3. Ensure clean drinking water with a WATER FILTER
4. Water canister for water supply
5. Tablets/powder, to make the water last
6. Sleeping back for COLD NIGHTS
7. Ground sheets or sleeping mats
8. Bivouac sack
9. Small mosquito net(!)
10. Where possible tarpaulin (no tent), cords, tent pegs
11. Earplugs (sleep is IMPORTANT!)
12. Gas cooker and gas cartridges AND/OR wood burner (small)

13. Things to make fire with
14. Glasses! Get a spare pair and keep them safe!
15. Folding toilet (can't flush a toilet without electricity!)
16. Candles as a source of light
17. SACRED CANDLES (3*) and black paper (4*) for the windows (provision: three days of darkness)
18. Curd soap and all hygiene articles (e.g. cookable and washable fabric toilet paper and fabric sanitary napkins!)
19. Handkerchiefs (boil-proof)
20. Automatic wristwatch or one with manual winding (without battery, preferably with date display)
21. Compass
22. Chamois leather as a "towel" or small microfibre cloths - they actually do and are easy to store
23. Canned food, dried fruit, flour, rice for at least 3 weeks

24. **Stockpile important medication!**

I personally recommend the following:

- Test the sleeping bag outdoors (... very important: with mosquito net!)

- Test: Stretch out the tarpaulin

- Collect firelighters and small wood in the forest, make a fire (please on your own property!): Start up the wood gas stove

- Collect wild herbs (especially the medicinal plants nettle and ground elder, which are particularly valuable in times of war) and cook simple dishes.

Building a tarp requires – like many other things –
PRACTICE...;–)
You can set it up high or keep it low when it rains – in
any case, the "closed side" to the west or north
(weather side).

MY VISIONS

In 2016, I had an inspiration during a prayer:

**"*2021 there will be a war in Germany.*
Warn everybody you know.".**

I was very hesitant about it. I had never received "predictions about world events", so I knew very little about them.

In January of this year (2020), I was "whispered" that potatoes and grain might become scarce in Germany next year.
So that you can weather the storm relatively well and DON'T GO HUNGRY, people should...

1. ... buy corn flour (Masa Harina!) in order to be able to bake thin flat cakes, which can then be filled with everything that is currently available (vegetables, herbs, possibly also meat).
2. ... buy a manual yogurt maker so that you can make your own yogurt with milk and a little boiled water. That would, especially in terms of immune-boosting aspects, ensure

that you could "somehow survive" the whole thing. (... provided, of course, that you have also stocked up on yogurt cultures!)

3. ... ALWAYS place water next to violet light before using it. (...for cleaning? Violet light should kill germs.) If there is no more electricity for a coloured light lamp, then people should use a purple film through which the water would be "violet irradiated" by sunlight...

Are we really facing famine? And, if yes, how?

Is there a connection between the prediction: "War in 2021" and the nutritional recommendations...???

Closing Remarks

I personally would not believe Alois Irlmaier's prophecies if... I had read them "by accident". Although I am a medium, I would also have my doubts because... I cannot imagine something like this happening. And that brings us back to the "Cassandra Syndrome"! ;-)
That's why I understand my friends' mostly uniform reaction to my early warning in 2016: "That's impossible!".

But I hear it loud and clear:

"In 2021, There Will Be a War in Germany".

No "...there COULD be a war". It was clear as day in my consciousness....

I can't "get visions on command", otherwise I'd do it now. Specific information "comes" to me at certain times and it normally pertains to my own life. Up to now, for more than 40 years, all of THESE visions have come to fruition. And now that I am moving to the "foreign terrain of the forecast of world events", should that be different??

I have done EXTENSIVE research! Since collapsing at home in front of my garden gate on 30 April, I have turned all the information I've been able to get over and over in my head. Increasingly, I am CONVINCED that all paths lead to Rome...

There is probably nobody who can say with certainty whether such a scenario will exist in "our time". But you can be sure: if it is worth the work to write and publish this booklet and I take the risk of ridiculing myself with this possibly "absurd-sounding" information, then... you can assume that it is IMPORTANT to inform you.

If NOTHING of everything that is written in this booklet arrives, I will go to celebrate with my loved ones with relief, eat my favourite pizza and enjoy my life...!

Then, in the best case, I/we will have learned a little more about "preparing for a crisis" and also about "sustainability", because everything that is used and needed in a war cannot be agreed with our "throwaway society".

However, this is my plea to you:

pay attention to world events - from a slightly different angle - and whatever you think is right and want to DO: DO IT SOON!

I wish for all of our sakes that these prophecies will never come true, regardless of whether they are "fixed" or "changeable" - I work as a precaution AND pray and hope for the best....

Yours, Tayala Léha.

PS: DATE?

My small book will be published soon... A date has been haunting my head for days:

13 August

Following my intuition, I checked the prophecy: August 13 falls in 2020 on Thursday, in 2021 on Friday...
I remember Irlmaier saying, **"The war will start in SPEYER (Germany) on a Friday between midnight and 2 am."**. The other prophet saw that **"the oats will be ready but there will no harvest."**. *(2*)*

Oats are usually harvested from mid-August. I wanted to know exactly... After phoning the Bavarian Ministry of Agriculture on 23 July 2020, I found out that: "The wheat will be harvested in the next two weeks and the oats in 2 to 3 weeks."! Bull's eye!
When the harvest be next year?

The "global crisis" that is expected to IMMEDIATELY precede the war and that has been predicted by many recognised clairvoyants may be the "coronavirus crisis".

Does the predicted event catch up with us in 3 weeks in 2020? Or should we expect the war next summer? Maybe we can escape the war too...? Nobody knows for sure.

I repeat: Pay close attention to "Irlmaier's SIGNS" and the current development of world events!
Take the "13 August" NOT literally for the sake of precaution, but I feel obliged to note the prompting with the date because... I can't get it out of my head...

Bibliography/Explanations

1* "Gaukler process", States Archives Munich/ BezA/LRA 208.026 – also accessible at www.alois-irlmaier.de (document overview)

2* Source: Book "Refugium" (Stephan Berndt)

3* "Sacred candles" belong to the sacraments consecrated by a priest. These candles should act as a "LIGHT" in various situations.

4* Black paper as a cover for all windows so that you CAN'T LOOK OUT or look in. Maybe nowadays tightly closing shutters could also work? In any case, all windows and doors should be blocked from light and view!

Recommended Reading

This book is also available in
a German printout.

ISBN 978-3-7504-9956-0

This is available in bookstores in
Germany, Austria and Switzerland
as well as in India, China,
South Korea, Brazil, England,
Australia, Canada and the USA.

CPSIA information can be obtained
at www.ICGtesting.com
Printed in the USA
BVHW061744050422
633412BV00004B/624